Notes / Ex

The Heart Of A Hero: Daily Devotionals for Christian Firefighters

Delightful Devotionals

CONTENTS

Introduction

In the dynamic world of firefighting, each day brings forth unique challenges and opportunities for courage. This 21-day devotional series is crafted to uplift and inspire the brave men and women who stand at the frontline, ready to confront the flames and uncertainties of their calling.

As firefighters, your commitment to service extends beyond the tangible—into the realm of the unseen challenges, emotional tolls, and the enduring spirit that defines your noble calling. These devotionals aim to provide a moment of reflection, a source of strength, and a connection to a higher purpose as you navigate the demands of your essential role.

Each day, you'll find a carefully selected Bible verse, a thoughtful reflection to ponder, journal questions to reflect on, and a heartfelt prayer to guide you. Whether you're just starting your firefighting journey or you're a seasoned hero, this devotional series is designed to be a beacon of hope, a reminder of your vital contribution, and a source of spiritual renewal in the face of adversity.

May these daily reflections serve as a source of inspiration, bringing light to your path and fortifying your spirit as you courageously stand in the line of duty.

Day 1: Courage Under Fire

Verse of the Day:

Joshua 1:9 (NIV) - "Have I not commanded you? Be strong and courageous. Do not be afraid; do not be discouraged, for the Lord your God will be with you wherever you go."

Reflection:

As a firefighter, navigating the intense heat of challenging situations is part of your calling. Amidst the flames and uncertainty, take a moment to draw strength from the unwavering courage that God commands.

Fear may surround you, but the Lord, your God, is a constant presence, offering courage and assurance in the face of danger. The flames may roar, and uncertainty may linger, but let your heart find peace in the unwavering courage that stems from Your God.

As you stand in the face of danger, may your faith be the shield that guards your spirit, and may the assurance of God's constant companionship be the flame that lights your way through the challenges that lie ahead.

Journal:

1. When have you felt the need for courage in your role as a firefighter?

2. How does your faith influence your approach to challenging situations?

3. Consider a moment when you overcame fear. What role did your faith play?

Prayer:

Almighty God, grant me the strength and courage to face the challenges that come my way. In the midst of the flames, be my guiding light, dispelling fear and instilling confidence in Your unwavering presence. Amen.

Day 2: Hope in the Flames

Verse of the Day:

Romans 12:12 (NIV) - "Be joyful in hope, patient in affliction, faithful in prayer."

Reflection:

In the challenging and often intense environment you face as a firefighter, cultivating hope becomes a powerful anchor. Romans 12:12 encourages a spirit of joy in the midst of hope, patience in affliction, and faithfulness in prayer. As you confront the flames, let this verse be a reminder that hope is not extinguished by adversity but can flourish even in the heat of the moment.

Amidst the chaos and uncertainty, envision joy as a resilient flame that burns within, fueled by the hope that persists despite the challenges.

Let patience be your ally in the face of affliction, a steady force that withstands the tests of the flames. And in the quiet moments, let faithfulness in prayer be your connection to a source of strength that goes beyond the visible and tangible.

As you navigate the challenges of your duty, may this verse be a guiding light—a reminder that hope is not a fragile entity easily extinguished by the intensity of the environment. Instead, it is a force that thrives amidst adversity, providing you with the endurance, resilience, and optimism needed to confront the flames with a spirit fueled by joy, patience, and unwavering faith.

Journal:

1. How do you maintain hope in challenging situations as a firefighter?

2. In what ways has patience played a role in your firefighting experiences?

3. Reflect on a moment when your faithfulness in prayer brought comfort during adversity.

Prayer:

Gracious God, in the midst of challenges, help me find joy in hope, patience in affliction, and faithfulness in prayer. May the flame of hope burn bright, lighting the way in the darkest moments. Amen.

Day 3: Facing Fear

Verse of the Day:

Psalm 34:4 (NIV) - "I sought the Lord, and he answered me; he delivered me from all my fears."

Reflection:

Fear is a natural response in the face of danger, yet Psalm 34:4 assures us that seeking the Lord brings deliverance from all fears. As a firefighter, you encounter situations that evoke fear, but trusting in God's presence and seeking His guidance can provide strength to overcome those fears.

In the midst of challenging circumstances, where danger looms and uncertainties abound, Psalm 34:4 becomes a source of empowerment. It reminds us that, in turning to the Lord, we find deliverance from the grip of fear. As a firefighter, where courage is not the absence of fear but the triumph over it, this verse becomes a beacon of assurance.

As you step into the line of duty, let this verse be a whispered encouragement, reminding you that seeking the Lord not only delivers you from fear but also infuses you with the courage needed to navigate through the challenges you face. In trusting His presence, may you find the strength to confront fear head-on, emerging resilient and undaunted in the fulfillment of your noble role as a firefighter.

Journal:

1. Can you recall a specific instance where your faith helped you confront fear?

2. How do you cultivate trust in God's presence during challenging moments?

3. Reflect on the ways your faith has contributed to your courage as a firefighter.

Prayer:

Heavenly Father, grant me the strength to face fear with faith. In moments of uncertainty, be my source of courage and deliver me from all fears. Amen.

Day 4: Teamwork & Unity

Verse of the Day:

Ecclesiastes 4:9 (NIV) - "Two are better than one because they have a good return for their labor."

Reflection:

The challenges firefighters face often demand teamwork and unity. Ecclesiastes 4:9 emphasizes the strength found in companionship and collaboration. As you navigate the complexities of your duty, recognize the value of working together with your fellow firefighters, creating a bond that multiplies the impact of your labor.

Consider the weight of your responsibilities, the unpredictable nature of emergencies, and the need for swift, coordinated action. In these moments, the strength found in teamwork becomes a force multiplier.

A bond with your fellow firefighters, rooted in trust, mutual support, and shared goals, not only eases the burdens but also amplifies the impact of your collective efforts.

Journal:

1. How has the principle of "two are better than one" manifested in your firefighting experiences?

2. Reflect on a challenging situation where unity among firefighters made a significant impact.

3. How can you contribute to fostering a sense of brotherhood and unity within your firefighting team?

Prayer:

Heavenly Father, thank you for the strength found in unity. Guide us as firefighters to work together seamlessly, supporting one another for the greater good. Amen.

Day 5: Strength in Service

Verse of the Day:

Philippians 4:13 (NIV) - "I can do all this through him who gives me strength."

Reflection:

In the dynamic and challenging landscape of firefighting, where the demands are both physical and emotional, Philippians 4:13 serves as a guiding principle. The verse acknowledges that our strength is not solely reliant on our own abilities but finds its source in Christ Jesus.

Consider the moments when the weight of your responsibilities seems overwhelming, when physical strength alone may not be sufficient. It is in these instances that drawing on the divine strength outlined in Philippians 4:13 becomes transformative.

As a firefighter, aligning your mindset with this spiritual fortitude empowers you to face challenges with a courage that transcends the physical. Whether battling fires or offering support to those in distress, let the awareness of God's strength be the bedrock of your resilience.

Journal:

1. How has relying on God's strength impacted your ability to serve others in your firefighting career?

2. In what ways can you incorporate spiritual strength into your daily service as a firefighter?

3. Reflect on a specific instance where you felt God's strength guiding you in your duties.

Prayer:

Almighty God, grant us the strength to serve selflessly and courageously as firefighters. May your power sustain us in every situation. Amen.

Day 6: God's Protective Shield

Verse of the Day:

Psalm 91:4 (NIV) - "He will cover you with his feathers, and under his wings, you will find refuge; his faithfulness will be your shield and rampart."

Reflection:

In the midst of the intense and often perilous situations firefighters encounter, finding refuge and protection is paramount. Psalm 91:4 beautifully illustrates God's promise to shield and safeguard us.

As a firefighter, trust in the divine protection that envelops you, providing comfort and courage in the face of danger. Let God's faithfulness be your unwavering shield and fortress.

Allow the image of God's wings providing refuge to inspire a deep sense of trust and security. As you step into the line of duty, let this promise of protection be a source of comfort, instilling within you the courage needed to confront the perils that lie ahead.

Journal:

1. How does the imagery of God's protective wings resonate with you in your role as a firefighter?

2. Share a specific experience where you felt God's shield of protection in your firefighting career.

3. How can you incorporate a sense of divine refuge into your daily mindset as a firefighter?

Prayer:

Gracious God, we find refuge in Your wings, and we trust in Your protective shield. Be with us in every firefighting endeavor, shielding us from harm and guiding us with Your faithfulness. Amen.

Day 7: Crisis Leadership

Verse of the Day:

Proverbs 3:5-6 (NIV) - "Trust in the Lord with all your heart and lean not on your understanding; in all your ways submit to him, and he will make your paths straight."

Reflection:

In the dynamic and often unpredictable world of firefighting, where crisis management is a constant reality, Proverbs 3:5-6 offers invaluable wisdom. It advocates for wholehearted trust in the Lord and a reliance on divine understanding

Amidst the challenges of crisis management, submit your decisions and actions to God, allowing Him to guide your path. Seek divine wisdom to lead with courage, compassion, and discernment in the face of adversity.

Consider the weight of leadership in the midst of crises, where decisive actions and wise choices are paramount. Then, seek divine wisdom to lead with courage, compassion, and discernment in the face of adversity.

Journal:

1. How does trust in the Lord impact your decision-making during crises as a firefighter?

2. Share an instance where submitting to God's guidance brought clarity in a crisis.

3. In what ways can you incorporate Proverbs 3:5-6 principles into your crisis leadership approach?

Prayer:

Heavenly Father, guide us in crisis leadership and help us trust in You with all our hearts. May our paths be straight as we submit to Your wisdom and understanding. Amen.

Day 8: Compassion Amid Chaos

Verse of the Day:

Colossians 3:12 (NIV) - "Therefore, as God's chosen people, holy and dearly loved, clothe yourselves with compassion, kindness, humility, gentleness, and patience."

Reflection:

Amid the chaos and challenges you face as a firefighter, Colossians 3:12 serves as a poignant reminder of the divine virtues to embrace.

Clothing yourself with these divine virtues transforms not only your actions but also the atmosphere around you. It shifts the narrative from emergency response to an expression of God's love in action.

See, cultivating a heart of compassion transforms how you navigate the intensity of emergencies. You develop an empathy that goes beyond the flames and smoke, seeing the humanity in each person affected. Picture kindness as your uniform, a garment that softens the harsh edges of crisis and extends a helping hand.

Journal:

1. How does the concept of clothing yourself with compassion resonate with your experiences as a firefighter?

2. Share a specific instance where kindness or patience played a crucial role in a chaotic situation.

3. In what ways can you intentionally cultivate compassion in your daily interactions within the firefighting community?

Prayer:

Gracious God, help me embody compassion, kindness, and humility in the chaos of firefighting. Clothe me with virtues that reflect Your love and bring comfort to those in need. Amen.

32

Day 9: Faith Over Fear

Verse of the day:

Isaiah 41:10 (NIV) - "So do not fear, for I am with you; do not be dismayed, for I am your God. I will strengthen you and help you; I will uphold you with my righteous right hand."

Reflection:

Imagine the scenes where the air is thick with uncertainty, flames dance with unpredictability, and fear threatens to overwhelm. In those challenging moments, Isaiah 41:10 becomes more than words; it transforms into a source of strength and resilience.

Trusting in the promise that God is a steadfast companion, providing strength and support, becomes not just a choice but a lifeline.

In those critical junctures when uncertainty thickens the air, the assurance of His presence acts as a guiding light, cutting through the darkness of fear and instilling a profound confidence.

Embracing faith in the demanding landscape of firefighting isn't just a spiritual exercise; it's a practical necessity. It's the unwavering anchor that steadies your resolve, empowering you to face each daunting situation with a courage that emanates from trust in the divine promise of strength and support.

Journal:

1. How does the promise of God's presence and strength resonate with you in the context of firefighting?

2. Share an experience where choosing faith over fear made a tangible difference in your response to an emergency.

3. In what ways can you cultivate a mindset of faith in your daily life as a firefighter?

Prayer:

Heavenly Father, in moments of fear and uncertainty, I choose to trust in Your presence and strength. Uphold me with Your righteous right hand as I face the challenges of my calling. Amen.

35

Day 10: Endurance in Adversity

Verse of the Day:

James 1:12 (NIV) - "Blessed is the one who perseveres under trial because, having stood the test, that person will receive the crown of life that the Lord has promised to those who love him."

Reflection:

As a firefighter, trials, and challenges are inevitable. James 1:12 encourages you to endure with the knowledge that, through perseverance, you will receive a crown of life promised by the Lord.

Embrace the tests and trials as opportunities for growth, knowing that there's a spiritual reward in staying steadfast.

When you face the heat of these challenges, remember that enduring through them is not just a test of your skills but also an opportunity for inner growth. So, choose to tackle each challenge not just as a hurdle but as a chance to grow, knowing that the journey holds a deeper significance than the immediate struggles we face.

Journal:

1. How do you view trials and challenges in your firefighting career in light of James 1:12?

2. Share a specific instance where perseverance led to personal or professional growth.

3. In what ways can you encourage and support your fellow firefighters in enduring challenges?

Prayer:

Gracious Father, grant me the strength and endurance to persevere under trials, knowing that Your promises are true. May I find joy in the midst of challenges, trusting in the spiritual rewards You have prepared for those who love You. Amen.

Day 11: Light in the Darkness

Verse of the Day:

John 8:12 (NIV) - "When Jesus spoke again to the people, he said, 'I am the light of the world. Whoever follows me will never walk in darkness, but will have the light of life.'"

Reflection:

In the heart of challenging and dark situations, Jesus' promise of light and life serves as a guiding force for firefighters. Entrusted with the responsibility of facing adversity, you are called to embody that promise, bringing light and hope into moments of intense darkness.

Reflecting on this calling means considering how to be a source of light amid chaos, illuminating paths for others, and offering reassurance in times of uncertainty.

Whether through a steady presence or acts of bravery, you have the unique opportunity to radiate an internal light that dispels fear and uplifts those in need.

Journal:

1. How does the concept of Jesus as the "light of the world" inspire your role as a firefighter?

2. In what ways can you actively bring light and hope into challenging situations?

3. Share a personal experience where you felt the presence of light in a dark moment.

Prayer:

Lord Jesus, You are the light of the world. As I navigate through challenging situations, may Your light guide me and bring hope to those in need. Empower me to be a beacon of Your light in the darkness. Amen.

Day 12: Serving with Sacrifice

Verse of the Day:

Mark 10:45 (NIV) - "For even the Son of Man did not come to be served, but to serve, and to give his life as a ransom for many."

Reflection:

Jesus came not to be served but to serve. In your role as a firefighter, embrace the spirit of sacrifice in your service to others. Consider the ways in which your actions reflect a heart willing to give for the well-being and safety of those around you.

Much like Jesus' selfless service, your commitment to firefighting involves a readiness to put the needs of others before your own. Whether rushing into a burning building, providing medical assistance, or offering support in times of crisis, you recognize that true service involves a willingness to sacrifice personal comfort for the greater good.

In each act of service, strive to embody the essence of selflessness, understanding that, like Jesus, your purpose is to serve and make a positive impact on the lives of those you are called to help and protect.

Journal:

1. How does the idea of sacrificial service resonate with your role as a firefighter?

2. In what specific ways can you incorporate the spirit of sacrifice into your daily service?

3. Share an experience where sacrifice played a significant role in your firefighting duties.

Prayer:

Lord, help me embody the spirit of sacrificial service, following the example set by You. May my actions reflect a heart devoted to the well-being and safety of others. Amen.

Day 13: Finding Peace in Chaos

Verse of the Day:

Philippians 4:7 (NIV) - "And the peace of God, which transcends all understanding, will guard your hearts and your minds in Christ Jesus."

Reflection:

Amidst the chaos of unpredictable and intense moments, discover solace in the promise of God's peace. As a firefighter navigating through tough situations, invite the peace that surpasses understanding to guard your heart and mind.

Take a moment to reflect on how cultivating this inner peace can impact your responses to the challenges inherent in your role. Picture the scene – the unpredictability, the intensity – and imagine anchoring yourself in the peace that God provides.

It becomes a shield, guarding against the stress and turmoil that seeks to overwhelm you. In those critical seconds when split-second decisions matter, a heart and mind grounded in God's peace can make all the difference. It enables you to approach challenges with clarity, resilience, and a steadiness that transcends the external turmoil.

Journal

1. How do you currently cope with chaos and stress in your role as a firefighter?

2. In what ways can you intentionally seek God's peace in the midst of challenging situations?

3. Share an experience where the peace of God had a discernible impact on your firefighting duties.

Prayer:

Heavenly Father, in the midst of chaos, grant me Your transcendent peace. Guard my heart and mind as I navigate the challenges of my role as a firefighter. Amen.

Day 14: Resilience in Crisis

Verse of the Day:

Romans 5:3-4 (NIV) - "Not only so, but we also glory in our sufferings, because we know that suffering produces perseverance; perseverance, character; and character, hope."

Reflection:

As a firefighter, you are no stranger to adversity. Every call, every fire, and every emergency presents an opportunity to strengthen your resolve and deepen your well of resilience.

Reflect on the times when hope emerged from the darkest moments, serving as a beacon that pushed you forward. Recognize that your journey is not just about the physical demands of the job but an ongoing process of personal and professional development.

In acknowledging the transforming power of challenges, you not only fortify your own spirit but also become a source of inspiration for those around you. Through your perseverance and resilience, you embody the unwavering spirit of a firefighter.

Journal:

1. How have past challenges in your firefighting career contributed to your resilience?

2. In what ways can you encourage resilience in your fellow firefighters during difficult times?

3. Reflect on a situation where your perseverance led to positive outcomes.

Prayer:

Heavenly Father, in the midst of challenges, grant me resilience. May perseverance, character, and hope be cultivated in my firefighting journey. Amen.

Day 15: Guardians of the Community

Verse of the Day:

Proverbs 24:11 (NIV) - "Rescue those being led away to death; hold back those staggering toward slaughter."

Reflection:

As a firefighter, you are not just an individual with a job; you are a dedicated guardian entrusted with the safety and well-being of the community. Think about the weight of that responsibility and how each call to action holds the potential to make a life-altering difference for someone in need. Your role extends beyond immediate emergencies; it embodies a commitment to serving and safeguarding those around you.

Reflect on the selflessness inherent in your duty. The moments when you rush into danger, not for personal gain but to rescue and protect others, underscore the depth of your commitment. It's a profound act of courage that goes beyond the physical demands of the job; it speaks to the very essence of being a guardian – someone willing to put the needs of the community above their own.

Consider the impact of your selfless actions on the lives you touch. The reassurance you provide, the lives you save, and the protection you offer during crises create a ripple effect, influencing the fabric of the community you serve.

Journal:

1. How does your role as a firefighter align with the concept of being a guardian of the community?

2. Reflect on a specific rescue or protection mission. How did it impact your perspective on your role?

3. In what ways can you further enhance your commitment to being a guardian of the community?

Prayer:

Heavenly Father, grant me the strength and courage to fulfill my role as a guardian of the community. May I be guided by Your wisdom as I strive to rescue and protect those in need. Amen.

Day 16: Strength for the Weary

Verse of the Day:

Matthew 11:28 (NIV) - "Come to me, all you who are weary and burdened, and I will give you rest."

Reflection:

Today's verse, Matthew 11:28, speaks directly to the fatigue and burdens that may weigh heavily on your shoulders. "Come to me, all you who are weary and burdened, and I will give you rest."

Firefighter, in the midst of the challenges you face, this invitation extends beyond the physical demands of your profession. It's an open call to find peace and rejuvenation in a higher source of strength.

When the weight of exhaustion feels overwhelming, consider the promise of rest that comes from turning to this divine invitation. In those moments of weariness, recognize that there is a place to find respite and renewal, a sanctuary where burdens are lifted, and strength is restored.

As you navigate through the demanding days, find reassurance in the promise that, by turning to a source beyond yourself, you will discover the strength needed to endure and overcome. You are not only a firefighter on the frontline but also an individual deserving of rest and renewal.

Journal:

1. How do you typically cope with feelings of weariness and exhaustion?

2. Reflect on a specific instance when seeking God's rest provided you with renewed strength.

3. In what ways can you incorporate moments of rest and reliance on God into your firefighting routine?

Prayer:

Heavenly Father, I come to You in moments of weariness, seeking Your rest and strength. Grant me the resilience to face challenges with a rejuvenated spirit. Amen.

Day 17: Wisdom in Decision-Making

Verse of the Day:

James 1:5 (NIV) - "If any of you lacks wisdom, you should ask God, who gives generously to all without finding fault, and it will be given to you."

Reflection:

In the midst of those crucial decisions where split-second choices are your daily bread, recognize the incredible need for divine wisdom. This verse is a direct invitation to acknowledge that wisdom isn't a scarce commodity; it's generously given by God Himself—no strings attached.

As you bear the weight of responsibility in your noble profession, where decisions can shape destinies in an instant, choose to turn to the ultimate wellspring of wisdom. Embrace the assurance that, by seeking divine wisdom, you tap into an unerring and limitless source.

In those moments when clarity is your lifeline and choices echo with significance, trust that you can call upon a wisdom beyond your own understanding.

Journal:

1. How has seeking God's wisdom influenced your decision-making in the past?

2. Are there specific areas in your firefighting role where you recognize the need for divine guidance?

3. How can you cultivate a habit of seeking God's wisdom in your daily decision-making?

Prayer:

Heavenly Father, grant me the wisdom to make sound decisions in the challenges I face as a firefighter. May Your guidance be a beacon of light in moments of uncertainty. Amen.

Day 18: Healing in Service

Verse of the Day:

Luke 10:9 (NIV) - "Heal the sick who are there and tell them, 'The kingdom of God has come near to you.'"

Reflection:

Recognize the profound impact of healing that emanates from your service as a firefighter. Take a moment to reflect on how your actions extend beyond the immediate response to emergencies, contributing to a profound sense of hope and restoration in the lives of those you serve.

As a firefighter, you are not only a responder to crises but also a harbinger of healing in the aftermath. Picture the scenes where, amidst chaos and uncertainty, your expertise, compassion, and quick response serve as a beacon of hope.

Whether it's rescuing someone from a perilous situation or providing critical medical care, your actions become instrumental in alleviating suffering and fostering a path toward recovery.

Journal:

1. In what ways do you see your role as a firefighter contributing to the healing of those you serve?

2. How does the idea of bringing the kingdom of God near resonate with your understanding of service and healing?

3. Can you recall a specific moment where you witnessed the impact of your service on someone's well-being?

Prayer:

Gracious Father, guide me in bringing healing to those I serve as a firefighter. May my actions reflect the nearness of Your kingdom and bring comfort to those in need. Amen.

62

Day 19: Embracing Challenges

Verse of the Day:

1 Corinthians 16:13 (NIV) - "Be on your guard; stand firm in the faith; be courageous; be strong."

Reflection:

In the demanding landscape of firefighting, where challenges are as certain as the flames you confront, this verse serves as a steadfast beacon. It encourages you to be vigilant, stand firm in your faith, draw on courage, and embrace strength.

Amidst the complexities of your duty, envision faith as your unyielding foundation, a solid rock upon which you stand. In moments of uncertainty, let it be the anchor that steadies you. Picture courage as your unwavering companion, accompanying you through the thick of adversity. Whether facing towering flames or intricate emergency scenarios, let courage propel you forward, undaunted.

And in the face of physical and mental exhaustion, let strength be your shield, deflecting weariness and fortifying your resilience. Envision this strength not only in the physical demands of firefighting but also as an internal force that bolsters your resolve.

Journal:

1. How has your faith played a role in facing challenges in your firefighting journey?

2. In what ways have you experienced courage manifesting during challenging situations?

3. Consider a specific challenge you've encountered. How can you apply the strength derived from your faith in overcoming it?

Prayer:

Heavenly Father, grant me the wisdom to face challenges with unwavering faith, courage, and strength. May Your presence be my constant source of assurance as I navigate the difficulties inherent in my role as a firefighter. Amen.

Day 20: Gratitude in Action

Verse of the Day:

1 Thessalonians 5:18 (NIV) - "Give thanks in all circumstances; for this is God's will for you in Christ Jesus."

Reflection:

Gratitude, as a cornerstone of your mindset, has the power to transform the way you approach your duties. Amidst the demanding and often intense nature of firefighting, a thankful heart becomes a lens through which you view your experiences.

It allows you to find appreciation for the moments of camaraderie with your team, the trust placed in your skills, and the opportunity to make a positive impact in the lives of those you serve.

In the face of challenging circumstances, a grateful perspective can act as a source of strength and motivation. It enables you to focus on what you can control, fostering a sense of resilience when confronted with the unpredictable nature of your profession.

Journal:

1. How do you actively practice gratitude in your role as a firefighter, especially during challenging times?

2. Reflect on a specific instance where expressing thanks made a difference in your outlook or the dynamics of your team.

3. In what ways does gratitude align with your understanding of God's will for you in Christ Jesus?

Prayer:

Heavenly Father, help me cultivate a heart of gratitude in the midst of challenging circumstances. May my thankfulness be a source of strength and encouragement for myself and those around me. Amen.

68

Day 21: Eternal Perspective

Verse of the Day:

2 Corinthians 4:18 (NIV) - "So we fix our eyes not on what is seen, but on what is unseen since what is seen is temporary, but what is unseen is eternal."

Reflection:

As a firefighter, take a moment to ponder how adopting an eternal perspective can profoundly influence your approach to challenges and uncertainties. Adopting an eternal perspective means looking beyond the immediate challenges and uncertainties of your firefighting role.

Focusing on what is unseen invites you to look beyond the tangible aspects of your service and acknowledge the intangible impact you have on lives. It involves recognizing the lasting significance of your efforts, even when immediate results may not be apparent.

This shift in focus can contribute to a resilient spirit that persists through adversity, knowing that your service is part of something greater than the moment.

Journal:

1. How does the concept of an eternal perspective resonate with your role as a firefighter?

2. Can you recall a specific instance where focusing on the eternal influenced your response to a challenging situation?

3. How might adopting an eternal perspective bring a sense of purpose and resilience to your daily service?

Prayer:

Gracious God, help me fix my eyes on the eternal as I navigate the challenges of my role as a firefighter. May my service reflect the lasting impact of your love and grace. Amen.

Conclusion

As we conclude this 21-day journey, take a moment to reflect on the strength, resilience, and unwavering commitment that define your calling.

Each day, we've explored themes of courage, unity, compassion, and the profound impact of faith in the face of challenges.

In the demanding world of firefighting, you embody the spirit of selfless service and sacrifice. Your dedication to protecting and serving your community is a testament to the values that guide you—values rooted in courage, compassion, and an unyielding sense of service.

As you face the uncertainties that each day may bring, remember that you are not alone. The same faith that has guided you through this devotional series is a steadfast companion in the field.

May these reflections continue to inspire and uplift you, serving as a reminder that, even in the midst of the flames, there is a source of strength beyond what is seen.

Thank you for your unwavering commitment to being a hero in every sense of the word. May your spirit remain resilient, your courage unwavering, and your faith unshakable as you continue to serve with dedication and honor.

With warmest wishes and gratitude,

Delightful Devotionals

www.ingramcontent.com/pod-product-compliance
Lightning Source LLC
Chambersburg PA
CBHW061357140726
47997CB00003B/1251